Eleanor of Aquitaine
The First Grandmother Of Europe

by
John G. Gurley

Illustrated by Jim Martinez

authorHOUSE®

AuthorHouse™
1663 Liberty Drive
Bloomington, IN 47403
www.authorhouse.com
Phone: 1 (800) 839-8640

Published by AuthorHouse   02/04/2016

ISBN: 978-1-5049-7581-0 (sc)
ISBN: 978-1-5049-7580-3 (e)

Library of Congress Control Number: 2016901771

Print information available on the last page.

Introduction

When I retired from my teaching job at Stanford University 28 years ago, I told my wife, Yvette, that I wanted to spend my time with her and study what interested her, which was the French language, Paris, and everything else that was French. My plan was to give up economics, which I had been studying, teaching, and researching for over 40 years, and try to learn something new, in the area that claimed the attention of my wife. I did not wish to become a fossil in the economics

department by hanging on to my office and trying to keep up

with the new hot shots around me. My wife's interests were

much more appealing.

In the next few years, I did pretty well, with the help of

Yvette, in learning to read French, especially in the area of

history. At some point in these early retirement years --and,

perhaps, Yvette suggested it -- I ran across references to Eleanor

of Aquitaine. I was fascinated by the fact that, during her

lifetime, she was both the Queen of France and the Queen of

England. Imagine that! How could that be? Yvette knew only a little about this, so I began looking into her life and telling

Yvette almost daily what I was discovering.

It took me quite a while to find out that Eleanor, while born

in the 1100s, had direct descendants who were very famous in

the 1500s. This probably meant that her children and

grandchildren had become kings and queens across Europe, and

they in turn led directly, in the 1500s, to Henry VIII, Francis I,

Charles V, and the Holy Roman Emperor, Maximilian I. Of

course, Eleanor's genes marched on from there, right down to

the present day, for our own Queen Elizabeth of England is a direct descendant of Eleanor. I decided, however, to limit my

story at the 1500s.

Yvette encouraged me to begin writing this down. One day

in San Francisco, we were in Books, Inc. where I discovered two

large, beautiful notebooks, both with elegant blank pages.

Hundreds of pages just waiting to be written on. These were the

days before computers, but certainly not before typewriters.

Why didn't I simply purchase typing paper and begin typing out

the story of Eleanor? Good question. Instead, right there, in front

of those gorgeous, inviting notebooks, I decided to write out the story with pen and ink. Which I did, as the years went by, and as even more years went by. And still more.

At last, on page 403, I finished. Over 400 pages, covered with my handwriting, in pen and ink, certainly legible, but also definitely unreadable because of the massive amount of detail I found impossible to leave out. A wonderful story about Eleanor of Aquitaine and her descendants that absolutely no-one would read. The two voluminous notebooks also weighed several pounds, which was another mark against this otherwise marvelous work of history -- and, indeed, of art itself. Yes, it was a work of art, without any doubt. A work of art, the value of which was zero.

Well, I put it to one side, eventually forgot it, while Yvette and I continued taking trips to Paris, to areas like Grasse where her father was born and grew up, before he migrated to America. We lived for months in apartments of friends, in Paris and around Grasse in southern France. Yvette was in touch with cousins and older relatives, and we had many happy days with them.

Then, in 2005, when we moved from our campus home of 45 years to the nearby retirement home, now called Vi at Palo Alto, I discovered the two notebooks that I had put to one side almost 10 years earlier. In our new apartment, I carefully placed them in a bookcase where I was bound to see them from time to time.

About 3 years ago, right after I was compelled to yield my dear wife to a Memory Support unit in the adjacent Care Center, I turned at nights, hoping to forget my grief, to the task of simplifying, shortening, and rewriting the Eleanor story. This I did in a few months, with the aid of my new iPad. But once again, I put it to one side, for I soon became involved in writing about Yvette, and our (Carmen Galindo's and my) efforts to give my wife the happiest life that circumstances and our abilities allowed.

Although we believe we had much success in doing this, in the end the Dementia Beast had the last word, and our sweetheart was gone. I wrote one more book about Yvette's final five months, as a most remarkable period in which she became more beautiful than she had ever been, displayed more courage and more good humor than anyone had the right to expect.

Then I turned back, still once again, to the Eleanor story. I did some more rewriting and shortening. I decided that the book needed pictures of the principal characters. However, the drawings and portraits that I found were covered by copyrights and it would be fruitless or, at best, tedious to get permission to use them. Carmen knew a young man, Jim Martinez, who drew beautifully, and we succeeded in engaging him to give us original drawings of Eleanor, Henry VIII, and several other notables, all based on portraits and other drawings that can be found most anywhere.

Okay, that did it. So here's the illustrated, shortened, and simplified story of Eleanor and her marching genes over four centuries. I hope you like it.

ELEANOR OF AQUITAINE: THE FIRST GRANDMOTHER OF EUROPE

Chapter 1

The Four Monarchs

The Holy Roman Emperor, Maximilian I, died in 1519. The three most powerful leaders in Europe vied for the Emperor's vacant throne: Henry VIII, king of England, who was greatly interested but had little or no chance; Francis I, king of France,

who spent a small fortune in his attempt to obtain the post; and

Charles I of Spain, who was king and the grandson of

Maximilian I, and who, with even more money spent for bribes

on his behalf, won the exalted chair. Thus, Charles I, king of

Spain, became, at the same time, Charles V, Holy Roman

Emperor.

Shortly before his death, Emperor Maximilian I did

everything he could to ensure this outcome. Seven electors were

to decide this: the archbishops of Trier, Mainz, and Cologne; the

king of Bohemia; the count palatine of the Rhine, the duke of

Saxony, and the margrave of Brandenburg. These seven electors

chose the king of the Romans, who became the emperor-elect.

The Pope then confirmed this king as the Holy Roman Emperor.

Maximilian gave money, gifts, and promises to the electors

(except to the duke of Saxony, who apparently was above

corruption). Just before his death, Maximilian believed that he

had five of the seven electors "in his pocket". But after

Maximilian's death, the electors, in a bid for more money,

reopened the market to supporters of Charles and the other two

contenders.

In the end, the Bank of the Fuggers, in the person of Jacob Fugger II (1459-1525), carried the day. Fugger loaned vast sums to Charles and helped him slip money under the table to the electors. Charles's stature as a Habsburg was also a big plus, especially since his competitors were a Frenchman and an Englishman.

The Fugger family was handsomely rewarded by Emperor Charles V, who granted them sovereign rights over their lands, the privilege of issuing their own money, and other spoils.

The Habsburgs were the ruling house of Austria from 1282 to 1918. Charles V was the sixth Habsburg to be Holy Roman Emperor. His grandfather and great-grandfather preceded him. The three together were emperors for 118 years. The Holy Roman Empire, a successor of Charlemagne's empire, endured from 962 to 1806. It and the Habsburgs became almost as one from the 1430s onward.

Now what is astonishing about all of this is that Maximilian and the three monarchs wanting his throne, all four of them, were direct descendants -- that is, blood relations -- of Eleanor of Aquitaine, who was born four centuries before these events.

There she was, born in southwestern France, in 1122. And there they were, four centuries later, the four greatest monarchs of the time, and all in the Eleanor family.

Not only that, but all the early spouses of these monarchs were also direct descendants of Eleanor. Maximilian's first wife, Mary (Marie) of Burgundy, who died tragically at an early age, carried Eleanor's genes. The same was true for the first and second wives of Francis I -- Claude of France and Eleanor of Portugal -- the first wife of Henry VIII, Catherine of Aragon; and Isabella of Portugal, the only wife of Charles V. All of these royal women of the late 1400s and early 1500s were members of

16

the family of Eleanor of Aquitaine. Four monarchs and five queens (one empress) -- so far. More to come.

Mary of Burgundy, the Empress, was a headstrong woman, who loved hunting so much that, a few days after her marriage, she brought her hawks into her bedroom. Despite an advanced pregnancy, she went hunting one day. Her horse tripped in a hole and threw her against a tree. She was dead in hours, at the young age of 25. She had married Maximilian, after her father's death, not out of some dynastic consideration, but because she was in love with him.

Isabella of Portugal, the only wife of Charles V, died at the age of 36, after only 13 years of marriage. Charles was deeply in love with her, and upon her death, he went into solitude and mourning for seven weeks. He never forgot her, did not marry again, and on his death-bed, 19 years later, held her crucifix to his lips, then pressed it to his chest. This, despite the fact that, in 13 years of marriage, he was "home" less than half the time. This is a "warm" story, and unusual when other monarchs, left and right, were snapping up teenage girls for second and third wives.

Catherine of Aragon was a daughter of Queen Isabella and King Ferdinand, monarchs of Spain. She was the first wife, of six, of Henry VIII of England. She was married in 1509 and the marriage was annulled in 1533, after Catherine had given birth to 8 children, only one of whom -- a girl -- survived childhood. Henry's desire to divorce Catherine led to England's break with the Pope and Rome.

Henry VIII was the oldest of the three kings. Francis I was in the middle, and Charles V was the youngest, although they were all born within nine years of each other. These three monarchs ruled almost everything in western Europe and in

Spanish America. Charles V, in 1519, ruled Spain, Spanish America, the lands of Germany and northern Italy, the Habsburg lands in Austria and Hungary, the Netherlands, Luxemburg, Naples and Sicily, and other real estate. Francis I ruled over an enlarged and a unified France, for England had been almost entirely run out of the country by 1519. Henry VIII governed England and still had Calais on the French coast. He was only a few decades away from incorporating Wales into England and imposing a Protestant Church of Ireland in that land. Scotland would have to wait for incorporation into England until 1603.

There were some close relationships among the four monarchs. For example, Francis I in his second marriage chose the sister of Charles V, Eleanor of Portugal. This made the two monarchs, bitter enemies that they were, brothers-in-law. Also, Henry VIII married the sister of Charles V's mother, so that by marriage Charles was the nephew of uncle Henry. In fact, this is how they referred to each other. It should be noted, too, that the three kings, through their marriages, were all related to the Spanish monarchs, Ferdinand and Isabella.

We're going to encounter these relationships time and again. A son succeeds his father and stays where he is. But a daughter of royalty moves, often at a very early age and to a foreign country to marry the king there. Females fly every which way, while the males sit where they are. Since the choices are made within a limited range, the flying females are usually closely related to the stationary males. Consequently, it should cause us little surprise when Eleanor's genes continue on and on. And yet it is does bring us up short to learn that the present Queen Elizabeth of England is a direct descendant of Eleanor of Aquitaine. Almost 900 years intervene! You see, there's an exclamation mark, after I told you to expect such things.

Eleanor of Aquitaine

Chapter 2

The Life of Eleanor

Eleanor of Aquitaine was, first of all, Queen of France and then Queen of England. According to the London Times, she was the richest woman in the world throughout the millennium of 1000-1999. We might play it smart by paying some attention to her.

She was born either in 1122 or in 1124, either in Poitiers or in Belin Chateau near Bordeaux. I will work with 1122 and Belin Château. Eleanor came from a long line of dukes of

Aquitaine who were also counts of Poitiers, the first of whom can be traced to the 900s. Eleanor's grandfather, Duke William IX of Aquitaine (1071-1127), who has been called the first troubadour, composed verses and music about courtly love, which expressed sentiments that celebrated the knights' admiration of women and valued their own more gentle or less aggressive emotions. Courtly or courteous love was to the lady loved, usually sung to her from afar, often with little hope of a favorable outcome, especially if she were married or at a social rank or two above her admirer.

William IX's court, whether it happened to be in Poitiers, Bordeaux, or Toulouse, was often enlivened by poets and musicians, and occasionally by story-tellers, dancers, acrobats, jesters, or mimes. The most brilliant court was at Poitiers, which also had schools for teaching privileged young ladies poetry, music, and other liberal arts. William IX's court, however, also indulged in bawdy and naughty songs, and the duke himself was what we would now call a womanizer of the first rank. When not chasing women, he was on a Crusade to the Holy Land chasing infidels, though he had much more success with the former than with the latter.

King Louis VII of France

The son, William X, also presided over a brilliant and cultured court, in which the virtues of generosity and courage were praised as the ultimate attributes of knights and cultured persons. When William X died of contaminated water in 1137, during a pilgrimage to the shrine of Santiago de Compostella in northwest Spain, he left two daughters, including Eleanor, who was scarcely 15 years of age.

The death of her father without a male heir made Eleanor duchess of Aquitaine and countess of Poitou (Aquitaine lying in the corner of southwest France was a duchy, and Poitou, lying north of it, was a county). These lands possessed by Eleanor were held at the will of the French crown, and so Eleanor herself

owed allegiance or homage to the king, who at that time was

Louis VI, called the Fat, then fast failing in health. Eleanor's

father had made her a ward of this king, who quickly saw the

advantages of arranging a marriage between his land-rich ward

and his sixteen-year-old son and heir. This event took place

almost immediately, so within a few months the death of Louis

VI made Eleanor the Queen of France and her husband, Louis

VII, the King. The year was 1137.

Eleanor and Louis took residence in the royal palace on the

Ile de la Cité in Paris. There she gave birth in 1145 to a

daughter, Marie. Two years later, she accompanied her husband

on a Crusade to the Holy Land, a disastrous enterprise that

ended without any notable victories over the infidels. Shortly

after returning home, Eleanor gave birth to a second daughter,

Alix (Alice). But by then her marriage was foundering, and

within a short time, in 1152, the two were separated by decree of

the Church, based on considerations of consanguinity (too close

a blood relationship). They were third cousins, once removed.

The "divorce" was a decision of great moment and one

made by Louis alone, for a woman could not make it, though

Eleanor no doubt urged it. It is difficult to imagine a king, deeply in love with his wife, as he was, and fully aware that he was dismantling a large part of France, since Eleanor would get her lands back, actually going through with the "divorce". This can only be explained by the deep religious feeling of Louis that his marriage was in fact invalid in the eyes of God -- a feeling that blinded him to all other considerations. Eleanor's famous remark that she thought she was marrying a king but found she had married a monk is certainly appropriate to her divorce: only a monk, not a king, would have divorced her! As we shall see, Louis's decision changed the course of French-English history over the next three centuries.

So after fifteen years of marriage, Eleanor's lands were returned to her. Her two young daughters, who were declared legitimate, were given to the father, and both Eleanor and Louis were allowed to remarry. Eleanor was now around thirty years of age. It can now be told that her desire to be free was owing to an attractive young man she met in 1151 -- Henry, son of Geoffrey IV, count of Anjou, who had the year before transferred his title of duke of Normandy to his son.

After the death of Geoffrey IV in 1151, and Eleanor's divorce the next year, young Henry and Eleanor wasted no time. Without obtaining permission from Louis VII, as they should have, they were married in 1152, only eight weeks after the divorce, she at the age of 30, he at only 19. Her vast land holdings were added to his, the consolidation now comprising Normandy, Anjou and Maine, Poitou, and Aquitaine, the last extending south through Gascony to Bayonne. These lands made up almost one-half of modern-day France, and at the time they far exceeded those held by the king of France.

About two years later, in 1154, Henry, a great-grandson of William the Conqueror, and a grandson of the former English king, Henry I, succeeded in gaining the English throne, and he, as Henry II, and Eleanor became king and queen of England.

Now all the French estates of the two became England's. In addition to the lands of England, Henry II soon controlled Scotland, Wales, Ireland, as well as Toulouse and Brittany. This "empire" completely overwhelmed the narrow lands in the kingdom of France. Could Louis VII have foreseen this and still have gone through with the divorce? But how could he have missed the grave consequences of his decision?

Eleanor's marriage to Louis VII had produced two daughters, Marie and Alix. In her marriage to Henry II , she gave birth to eight children, five boys and three girls. Altogether, then, Eleanor had five girls and five boys. Her first son, William, died at age three, but the rest of the children survived into adulthood, which is quite remarkable for that time. Eleanor's second son, Henry, died of dysentery at age 28. Her fourth son, Geoffrey, was killed in a tournament, also at the age of 28. Richard, her third son, became king of England in 1189 upon the death of his father, but he was killed ten years later in a minor battle before a chateau near Poitiers in France. This son became known as Richard Lion-Heart, owing to his military exploits. Eleanor's last son, John, succeeded Richard as king and held the throne for 17 years.

King Henry II of England

Aside from the ten births spanning 21 years, Eleanor was a patroness of the arts -- poets, singers, musicians -- at Poitiers, Paris, and London, an interest that was developed in her childhood and that may have been in her genes. Eleanor's cultural tastes were extended to the court of Castile by her daughter, Eleanor; to the court of Champagne at Troyes by her daughter, Marie; and to the French court by her granddaughter, Blanche -- a tale I will tell later -- and to the English courts by her sons, Richard and John. Richard was an accomplished composer of verse and music, and an enthusiastic chorister. John, too, shared Richard's passions.

Starting in the 1170s, some of Eleanor's sons began rebelling against their father, and Eleanor, who herself was becoming alienated from her husband, found herself siding with her sons. While Henry II usually forgave his sons for their bad behavior, he was harsh with his wife for her disloyal role. This led him, in 1174, to incarcerate Eleanor for most of each year over the next 15 years. Only on Henry's death in 1189 was Eleanor released from "house arrest" and at times from actual imprisonment, usually in the Chateau of Chinon.

In her later years, she toured England, releasing prisoners, passing laws making weights and measures uniform, and acting as head of state before the coronation of Richard. Still later, she

traveled from the Abbey of Fontevraud, just south of the Loire

valley, to the tip of Italy and then to Sicily to arrange a marriage

for King Richard since he was embarking on a hazardous

Crusade to the Near East still unwed -- and then back to the

Abbey of Fontevraud.

After Richard's capture during his return from the Holy

Land, she travelled extensively in England, and worked long

days, to help in gathering ransom money for his release as a

hostage, and then went to Germany with the money for the same end. Still later, she rushed miles to be at Richard's side when he was dying from wounds suffered in a minor skirmish.

Eleanor fought for her last son, John, as the successor to King Richard -- despite his treasonable behavior during Richard's reign -- partly by traveling to Aquitaine to make certain of John's support there. She went over the Pyrenees to Castile and back to arrange for the marriage of a granddaughter, Blanche, to the future Louis VIII of France. She was 78 years old when she made this round trip, overland.

Eleanor died on April 1, 1204 at the age of 82.

Chapter 3

England

The stage is set. On one side are Eleanor of Aquitaine, her second husband, Henry II, King of England, and their eight children. On that side we are in the 1100s. On the other side are the four monarchs, Henry VIII, Francis I, Charles V, and Maximilian I. We can add in their wives, and later other notables. On this side, the year is 1519. We will go from Eleanor on one side to the other side, telling stories as we proceed.

Let's begin with Henry VIII. How come he is a direct descendant of Eleanor? One thing we will learn is that it may be possible to go from Eleanor to one of the monarchs on the other side by more than one route. For example, Charles VI, King of France, was the great-great grandfather of Henry VIII, King of England. So we may be able to go from Eleanor through the kings of France down to Charles VI then swerve over into the English kings. However, it may also be possible to go first to "Spain" and then to the French kings. My plan is to keep things as simple as I can, though I do not want to pass up a good story. We will see how that plays out.

All right, how do we get in a simple but interesting way from Eleanor to Henry VIII? To begin with, two of Eleanor's sons were kings of England. That's a real good start. Richard succeeded his father in 1189 and reigned for 10 years. Eleanor's last child, John, became king in 1199 and was on the throne until 1216. Starting with John, here is a list of the kings of England down to Henry VIII, along with information about their birth-death and reign years, and the relation of each to his predecessor.

King John of England

King	Birth-Death.	Reigned.	Relationship
John	1167-1216.	1199-1216.	Brother
Henry III.	1207-1272.	1216-1272.	Son
Edward I.	1239-1307.	1272-1307.	Son
Edward II.	1284-1327.	1307-1327.	Son
Edward III.	1312-1377.	1327-1377.	Son
Richard II.	1367-1399.	1377-1399.	Grandson
Henry IV.	1366-1413.	1399-1413.	1st Cousin
Henry V.	1387-1422.	1413-1422.	Son
Henry VI.	1421-1471.	1422-1461.	Son
		1470-1471	
Edward IV.	1442-1483.	1461-1469.	3rd Cousin
		1471-1483	
Richard III.	1452-1485.	1483-1485.	Brother
Henry VII.	1457-1509.	1485-1509.	3rd Cousin, once removed
Henry VIII.	1491-1547.	1509-1547.	Son

There are double reign periods for two of the monarchs.

Henry VI was deposed by Edward IV in 1461, but Henry

returned briefly as king in 1470-1471, at which point Edward IV

once again was able to claim the throne.

We see that Eleanor's son, John, was followed by his son,

Henry III, who was in turn followed by his son, Edward I. This

Edward was the great-grandson of Eleanor of Aquitaine. Now

that looks simple: Eleanor-John-Henry III-Edward I; mother-

son-grandson-great grandson. Fine. We could now just continue on from there. However, if we did, we would be missing out on

some interesting stories involving mothers and daughters from

Spain and France. (Permit me to use "Spain" even though its

consolidation as such lies in the future.) Let's pause to have a

look at a few of these women and young girls.

Eleanor of Aquitaine had a namesake daughter, who at the

age of 9 left her mother to marry King Alfonso VIII of Castile,

this in 1170. This couple eventually had a daughter, Berenguela,

who in time married Alfonso IX of Leon. A son of theirs was to

become Ferdinand III of the united Castile and Leon. He in turn

had a daughter named Eleanor of Castile (1241-1290). Let's see where we are. Eleanor of Castile must be the great-great

granddaughter of Eleanor of Aquitaine. She was born 37 years

after the death of our Eleanor. This young Eleanor was named

after her great grandmother, Queen Eleanor of Castile, who was

the daughter of our Eleanor of Aquitaine. It's too bad that we

have three Eleanors here, but we will carry on as best we can.

There will be several more! Now, this newest Eleanor, when she

was only 13, was sent from her homeland to marry a 15-year-old

future king of England. Guess who? Yes, he would become

Edward I, King of England. So, why this story? Well these two

youngsters were both direct descendants of Eleanor of

Aquitaine. One was her great-great granddaughter, and the other was her great grandson. The two young people were second cousins once removed.

Once more: Eleanor of Aquitaine sends a daughter to Spain, campaigns to get a son in as king of England, and then years later from Spain comes a descendant of that daughter to marry a descendant of that son. This youngest Eleanor died at a rather young age, and this broke the heart of Edward I. The depth of their love can be imagined in one of the Eleanor Crosses that remains at Charing Cross in London. In French: Cher Alienor = Charing (Eleanor) Cross.

Pretty good, so far. On with the story. Eleanor of

Aquitaine's namesake daughter, who married Alfonso VIII of

Castile, had another daughter named Blanche (1188-1252). It

came to be decided that Blanche should marry the future Louis

VIII of France (1187-1226). When Eleanor of Aquitaine was 78

years old, she undertook this long journey overland, across the

Pyrenees, to fetch a granddaughter on the plains of Castile.

There she saw her own daughter for the first time in 30 years.

Queen Eleanor of Castile was now 39 years of age, but still

beautiful, a learned woman, gracious and pious. Her court was

culturally brilliant, filled with troubadours, poets, prelates, and grandees -- and why not, for she was the great granddaughter of William IX of Aquitaine, the first troubadour, and the daughter of our Eleanor who had treasured and furthered music and verse in her several courts. Our Eleanor found there three granddaughters of marriageable age, but she saw something special in the eyes and behavior of Blanche. So, after a short visit, Eleanor and Blanche managed the difficult climb back through the Pyrenees, then down onto the Gascony plain, and on to Bordeaux, where she and her granddaughter rested through the Easter holidays of 1200. From there they travelled north to the abbey of Fontevraud, located just below the Loire valley.

There Eleanor stopped, tired and ill, while her party continued

on with Blanche to Normandy, where the marriage took place on

May 23, 1200. (Remember that England was conquered by

William of Normandy only 134 years prior to this marriage.)

When Blanche and Prince Louis wed, she was perhaps 12

years old and he was 13. (Try to keep in mind that we are going

from Eleanor of Aquitaine to King Edward I of England, but this

time by way of both Spain and France. Our end goal is to get to

Henry VIII of England.). For another 23 years, this royal couple

remained princess and prince. At that point, King Phillip II died

at the age of 58. Louis then became king as Louis VIII, but his reign was for only three years, 1223-1226, for he died suddenly at the relatively young age of 39. During her marriage of 26 years, Blanche gave birth to 11 or 12 children. She was not only Queen of France but, after her husband's death, she was Régente of the kingdom, until 1234, when her young son reached adulthood.

Blanche was a beautiful woman who possessed an exemplary character from a religious point of view. She was widely admired for her untarnished virtue as wife and widow and for her devotion as mother to her many children. She had a strong religious influence on her son, Louis IX, who dedicated much of his life to the Church and so became a saint only a few decades after his death. Blanche spent large sums on charity, and she helped finance the building of the Chartres Cathedral. She and her son also founded the Abbey of Royaumont in 1228. In addition, they financed the building of Sainte-Chapelle in Paris, to house relics (of dubious authenticity) purchased by Louis IX. These relics cost three times the entire cost of building Sainte-Chapelle.

Blanche was a granddaughter of a Queen of France and England (our Eleanor), a daughter of a Queen of Castile, a wife of a King of France, and a mother of another King of France.

Interesting, but why are we discussing this woman? Because her son, Louis IX, had a son, who became King Phillip III of France (1245-1285), who in turn had a daughter, Marguerite of France (1282--1318). This Marguerite became the second wife of King Edward I, after his dear first wife, Eleanor of Castile, died in 1290.

All right, take a deep breath, and let it out slowly. Edward I of England was the great-grandson of our Eleanor of Aquitaine. Actually, that would be enough, and we could have proceeded on toward Henry VIII, our ultimate goal. But I decided to tell you a few stories of some remarkable women. One was Eleanor of Aquitaine's own namesake daughter, who became Queen Eleanor of Castile. In time, down this line in Spain, there appeared another Eleanor of Castile, a great-great granddaughter of our Eleanor. And this young girl became the first wife of King Edward I of England.

Now, let's take another deep breath. We have just gone from England down into Spain and then back to England. Now we are going to go from England down into Spain then up to France and from there back to England. Eleanor of Aquitaine's namesake daughter had a daughter, Blanche. Blanche was sent up to France to marry a future king of France. Eventually, there appeared a great (3)-granddaughter of Eleanor of Aquitaine,

who was sent back to England. (Great (3) means three greats.).

You see, girls are flying around, and the men are sitting on their

rumps.

Up to this point, I have discussed three Eleanors and a

Blanche. The number of children these four women had is

almost beyond imagination. Here are the counts:

King Edward III of England

Eleanor of Aquitaine	(1122-1204).	10
Eleanor, Queen of Castile	(1162-1211).	11 At most
Eleanor of Castile, Queen of England	(1241-1290)	16 At most
Blanche, Queen of France	(1188-1252).	12
	Total	49 At most

These four women may have given birth to 49 children. The true figure, however, lies between 44 and 49.

I have already noted that all but one of the children of Eleanor of Aquitaine lived into adulthood, though only two of them outlived her. But over a century later, only six of the 12-16 children of Eleanor of Castile lived past the age of 20. Blanche saw only four of her 12 children outlive her, though one other reached the age of 34.

So now, leaving these women and their children, we are with Edward I and his second wife, Marguerite of France. A son of Edward I became Edward II, King of England (1284-1327). A son of the latter became Edward III (1312-1377). Then a grandson of Edward III, who called himself Richard II, lived from 1367 to 1399. That gets us halfway through the list of English kings from John to Henry VIII.

To make things more interesting, let's back up. Edward II was a homosexual. But, of course, he had to marry, and this to an innocent young girl of 14 or 15. She learned very quickly that his amorous inclinations were directed not to her but to his boy-friends. Also she saw immediately that he had little interest in his duties as king and that he hung out, not with his counselors but with lower types, such as gamblers. Many of England's nobles formed an opposition to the king. Eventually, he was forced to abdicate his throne and imprisoned. The enemies of Edward II could not let him live, even as a prisoner, for he would always be there as a rallying point for his partisans. So

Edward was killed, presumably in a way as to conceal any violence against him. Although it is far from certain, it is said that the method chosen was a red-hot iron shoved through a cone far into his anus. However, this is a story that one would expect from those who disapproved of his homosexual activities. But it is likely true.

Now for another shock: King Edward had four children by his wife, Isabelle of France, daughter of King Philip IV of France. King Philip was the great (3)-grandson of Eleanor of Aquitaine, so Isabelle was our Eleanor's great (4)-granddaughter. Edward II was Eleanor's great-great-grandson.

So the married pair were third cousins, twice removed. That is probably more than you want to know, so let's go on.

This elder son grew up to become Edward III (1312-1377). He was crowned king in 1327 at the age of 15. The year before, Edward was betrothed to Philippa, countess of Hainault, who was probably about 13 years old, a match arranged by Edward's mother, Isabelle, partly for the dowry of Philippa. Philippa herself was a direct descendant of Eleanor of Aquitaine, through French kings. During her marriage, Philippa had 12 children, nine of whom survived infancy, five sons among them. The two oldest sons died before their father did. The middle son was

John of Gaunt, who at the death of his father stepped back in

favor of his nephew, the son of the eldest son of Edward III.

This 10-year-old became King Richard II. (Remember that

Richard I was our Eleanor's son, Richard Lion-Heart.)

Now John of Gaunt, who stepped back, had a son, who

eventually succeeded Richard II in 1399, at the age of 33,

calling himself Henry IV. (Our Eleanor married Henry II, and

their grandson was Henry III.). How are you doing? Henry IV

was the first cousin of the previous king. I hope that helps. The

son of Henry IV became Henry V, and his son became Henry

VI, who was crowned when he was 9 months old. We are now in the year 1422.

There are nine English kings from John to Henry VI, and eight of them had French wives. It was not until the latter half of the 1400s that English kings looked for English wives. That is to say, when the English were finally driven out of France (except for Calais), their kings looked inside their own country for their consorts. Remember, again, that England was conquered by the Normans (Normandy in France) in 1066. So naturally the "English" kings took French wives. It took four centuries for this practice to change. The language of the English court was French for at least 300 years after the Conquest.

Do you have another deep breath? Well, then, let's review how we got to Henry VI. Our Eleanor, her son, John, and his son, Henry III. (Remember that Eleanor's husband was Henry II.) Now son followed father through the three Edwards. We have our Eleanor's grandson, Henry III, then Edward I, II, and III, so Edward III would be Eleanor's great (3)-grandson.

Now we have to make way for a grandson and then a first cousin. The first two sons of Edward III died before he did. But a son of his eldest son was a 10-year-old when Edward III died,

and the dead king's third son stepped back in favor of this

youngster. That's how we get a grandson to follow Edward III.

This youngster took the name of Richard and so became Richard

II. He was forced to abdicate in 1399, was imprisoned, and was

probably murdered in prison the following year. He had no

children. Homosexuality very likely lay at the bottom of this

deed, as it did in the case of Edward II. Richard II's rival was his

first cousin, the son of John of Gaunt, third son of Edward III.

This first cousin became Henry IV in 1399.

Next, we have two sons following their fathers, Henry V and Henry VI. The latter was deposited on the throne, probably in diapers, when he was 9 months old, in 1422. We will stop here for a few moments.

How are you getting along? Perhaps the best thing you can do now is to check back to the list of English kings. Follow down from John to Henry VI. After John there are eight kings, and six of them were sons following their fathers. One was a grandson. And one was a first cousin. Thus, it is clear that down to Henry VI, Eleanor's genes are still marching on. Henry VI is Eleanor's great (7)-grandson.

King Henry VIII of England

Henry IV reigned from 1399 to 1413. He was immediately faced by a rebellion of barons who supported Richard II, but in a short time the rebels were rounded up and executed brutally. Triumphant against a second rebellion, Henry IV now appeared in command, but he also at the same time fell into ill-health. His eldest son gradually took charge of state affairs, but not without bitter quarrels with his father. Henry IV died in 1413 at the age of 47, an "old man" who, to the very end was guilt-ridden over the manner in which he usurped the throne, which probably involved the murder of his first cousin, Richard II.

His son, Henry V, was 26 years old when he became king.

He was 28 when his English army routed and destroyed the

French army at Agincourt (in northwestern France). He was 33

when he ruled both England and a good part of France, and he

was only 35 when he died. This king was immortalized by

Shakespeare. Henry VI, the son, started his kingship in the crib

and ended insane. He was murdered without an heir.

The next two kings were brothers, Edward IV and Richard

III, both great-great-grandsons of Edward III. Edward IV died of

a fever in 1483. His brother beat off other contenders and

became Richard III. This king then probably had his brother's two young sons murdered in the Tower of London. However, Richard's reign lasted only two years, for he was slain in a battle against the forces of Henry VII, who became king in 1485.

While Richard III had male ancestors back to Edward III, Henry VII's claim to the English throne was entirely different. His claim depended on his relationship to three women: his mother, who was the great-granddaughter of John of Gaunt (a son of Edward III); his paternal grandmother, Catherine of France, who was formerly queen of England; and his wife, Elizabeth of York, the daughter of a recent king of England.

Henry VII's claim was viewed as not bad, but not really strong, either, because only women were involved!

Henry VII and Elizabeth of York had several children. The oldest boy was Arthur, who was born in 1486 but died 16 years later of consumption. The future Henry VIII, the second son, was born in 1491, and it is he who closes out this chapter. He married his brother's widow, his sister-in-law.

Edward III is the pivotal figure here. Let's review once more. Edward III came to the throne at 15, then reigned for 50 years. He had four sons, and all of them had big families.

Edward's successor was a grandson, Richard II. Another grandson came next, Henry IV. A great-grandson and a great-great-grandson followed, as Henry V and Henry VI. Next came two more great-great-grandsons of Edward III, as Edward IV and Richard III. Finally, Henry VII was a great (3)-grandson, and Henry VIII was a great (4)-grandson of Edward III. Of course, Edward III himself was a direct descendant of Eleanor of Aquitaine, being her great (3)-grandson. So Henry VIII was our Eleanor's great (7)-grandson.

We made it! All we had to do was get to Edward III. He had grandsons and a variety of great-grandsons who followed him as kings of England.

I have a story left over. I hope you don't mind if I just throw it in here. Okay? Consider Richard II, who was a grandson of Edward III and reigned from 1377 to 1399. This Richard married twice but he had no children by these wives, which is not surprising for he was probably a homosexual and, moreover, his second wife was only 8 years old when he married her. Two strikes against having a kid. Richard's court group was criticized as effeminate, a "love not war" contingent. Since

Richard was only 10 when he was crowned, it took some years for him to gain power and influence. But, when he did, he turned on these critics and had them killed or exiled. So much for "love not war". One of them, the future Henry IV, son of John of Gaunt (third son of Edward III), came out of exile with an army -- provoked by the confiscation of all his lands by Richard in 1399 and by the extension to life of his banishment -- to defeat Richard's forces. The next year, the imprisoned king was probably murdered. And that is how another direct descendant of our Eleanor became a king of England.

When Eleanor became the Queen of England, she and her husband, King Henry II, ruled all of England and half of what is now France. When after 3 1/2 centuries we are with Henry VIII, we find that all the French lands are gone, except for Calais, on the France's coast across from Dover. We will look at this in the next chapter on French kings.

Chapter 4

France

The stage setting is still there. On one side we have Eleanor of Aquitaine and Henry II, queen and king of England, and their eight children. They are there in the 1100s. On the other side are the four monarchs: Henry VIII, Francis I, Charles V, and Maximilian I. On that side, it is 1519. Our task in this chapter is to move from Eleanor to Francis I, and show that the latter is a direct descendant of the former.

Let's do this fast to start with. Eleanor of Aquitaine, you will remember, traveled overland, across the Pyrenees, and into Spain, to get a granddaughter from the court of Castile, for marriage to the future King Louis VIII of France. This was the year 1200. They finally became monarchs in 1223.

After these two, there were 15 kings down to Francis I. In 10 cases, son followed father -- or, in one case (Louis IX), mother. In the other five, two brothers and three cousins were successors. When Charles IV died in 1328, the royal line shifted over to his first cousin, Philip VI. From this king, there were six father-son successions, down to Charles VIII (1470-1498), who died young in a tragic accident. Charles left no direct heir, so a second cousin (once removed) stepped in. When he left no heir, a first cousin (once removed) of his became Francis I.

Starting with Blanche, the granddaughter Eleanor brought back from Spain, here is a list of the 16 kings of France down to Francis I, along with information about their birth-death and reign years and the relation of each to his predecessor.

King-Queen.	Birth-Death.	Reign Years.	Relation
Blanche.	1185-1252.	1223-1226.	Granddaughter
Louis IX.	1214-1270.	1226-1270.	Son
Philip III.	1245-1285.	1270-1285.	Son
Philip IV.	1268-1314.	1285-1314.	Son
Louis X.	1289-1316.	1314-1316.	Son
Philip V.	1293-1322.	1316-1322	Brother
Charles IV.	1294-1328.	1322-1328.	Brother
Philip VI.	1293-1350.	1328-1350.	1st Cousin
John II.	1319-1364.	1350-1364.	Son
Charles V.	1338-1380.	1364-1380.	Son
Charles VI.	1368-1422.	1380-1422.	Son
Charles VII.	1403-1461.	1422-1461.	Son

Louis XI.	1423-1483.	1461-1483.	Son
Charles VIII.	1470-1498.	1483-1498.	Son
Louis XII.	1462-1515.	1498-1515.	2nd Cousin, once removed
Francis I.	1494-1547.	1515-1547.	1st Cousin, once removed

I have already related how Eleanor brought Blanche back from Spain to marry the future Louis VIII of France. Louis IX succeeded his father at the age of 12. For several years, as a minor, he ruled under the supervision of his mother, Blanche, who also imbued him with her own deep religious piety.

Louis IX, during a severe illness, vowed that, if he recovered, he would go on a Crusade to fight the infidels. He did recover and soon set forth in 1248 for the Holy Land. He was gone from France for six years, during part of which he was held a prisoner in Egypt, and part of which he spent in Syria fortifying French holdings there. His mother, who was again Régente in his absence, died before he returned. Later, Louis IX died of a plague while on a second Crusade.

Louis IX's oldest son, Philip III, became king in 1270 and ruled for 15 years. He in turn was followed by his own son, Philip IV, who was married in 1284 to Jeanne of Navarre-

Champagne, and these two lands were brought into the royal

domaine. Territorial expansion by marriage was followed by

territorial expansion by war into southwest France and into

Flanders in the north. While Philip IV achieved some success at

first, in the end he gained very little. However, Carcassone and

Aigues-Mortes, great fortress cities, were built during his reign.

Philip was instrumental in gathering together the first States-

General, an advisory parliament of sorts, in strengthening the

system of taxation, and in carrying out several devaluations of

the currency. Philip was also embroiled in violent controversy

with the Papacy, which resulted, however, in victory for him, when in 1309, a French Pope was elected and the Papacy itself was moved to Avignon, in southern France.

The three sons of Philip IV were married early. The eldest son, Louis X, wedded Marguerite of Burgundy in 1305 when he was 16 and she 12. His brother, Philip V, married Jeanne of Burgundy in 1307 when each was only 14. Finally, Charles IV married the younger sister of Jeanne, named Blanche, when he too was only 14 and she a year younger.

These three young ladies -- Marguerite, Jeanne, and Blanche -- were all involved in adulterous affairs, the first and third directly and the second as an accomplice. The Tour de

Nesle served as the locale for the affairs. This Tower was on the

left bank of the Seine, almost directly across the river from the

Louvre of the present day. There at night Marguerite and

Blanche met their lovers, the two brothers Gautier and Philip of

Aunay, with Jeanne acting as the go-between and look-out. This

went on for some time, but they were all eventually caught in

1314, charged and convicted of adultery or complicity in it.

Marguerite was imprisoned in the Château Gaillard where

she was strangled the following year. Blanche was also locked

up in the same Chateau then transferred to the Chateau of

Gournay, near Coutances in Normandy. After her marriage was annulled in 1322, she became a nun in the Abbey of Maubuisson. She was forced to give up a crown for a veil. Jeanne was convicted of complicity in the adulterous affairs and was imprisoned at Dourdan. She was pardoned and freed in 1315.

The two brothers were convicted in 1314 and executed the same year at Pontoise, just outside of Paris. Torture was part of the execution. Louis X, who became king in 1314 upon his father's death, remarried that same year. But Louis's reign lasted only 18 months up to his very early death in 1316. At that point his second wife was pregnant, and five months later she gave birth to a son, Jean I, who died in a few days -- or, perhaps, was murdered.

The next of the three brothers, Philip V, became king in 1316, and reconciled with his wife, Jeanne. Philip and Jeanne had seven children. Only two were boys, and both died shortly after birth. Philip V died in 1322 without a male heir, only six years after he was crowned.

The third brother, Charles IV, having repudiated his marriage to the convicted adulteress, Blanche, remarried in 1322 the daughter of the Emperor of the Holy Roman Empire. But she died two years later in childbirth. Charles then married once again, in 1325, and had three girls before he died in 1328, having had only six years as monarch.

Let's go back. Philip IV died in 1314. He had three sons. Each one became a king of France. However, only 14 years later, all three sons were dead, and there was no male heir from any of them. Five boys had died in their infancy. Also three wives were dead by this time. Yes, children remained but, damn it, they were all girls!

Blanche of Castile, Queen of France

What to do? Well, Philip IV, who had the three ill-fated sons, also had a brother, Charles, count of Valois. This count had a son who became the next king of France, under the name Philip VI. He was crowned in 1328, reigned for 22 years, dying in 1350. Philip VI was the first cousin of the three sons of Philip IV.

Are you still with me? One thing is clear: we are still speaking of French kings who were direct descendants of our Eleanor. From Eleanor's granddaughter, Blanche, we have had four sons of their predecessors, two brothers, and a first cousin. Eleanor's genes are still marching on.

We are at Philip VI in 1328. An interesting sidelight is that this Philip had to seize the throne. Not because there was a close competitor in France, but because there was one in England! That was Edward III, who had come to the English throne in 1327, a year before at the age of 14, and had a strong claim on the French throne. Edward III's mother was the daughter of Philip IV -- the same Philip with the three ill-fated sons and with a brother whose son became Philip VI. But that made Edward III of England a grandson of Philip IV, just as Philip VI was a grandson, too. The two contestants for the French throne were first cousins, once removed. However, Edward III was disadvantaged in that his claim was based on a woman -- his mother. Further, he was born in England, not France. Also, he was very young. In any case, at that point in 1328, Edward did not press his claim, and Philip of Valois seized the throne as Philip VI.

Philip VI was king from 1328 to 1350. After him, son followed father six times, down to Charles VIII, who reigned from 1483 to 1498. You can check this out by looking at the list of French kings near the beginning of this chapter. Charles VIII died young in a tragic accident, leaving no male heir. So a second cousin, once removed, took over, calling himself Louis

XII. He was the great-grandson of Charles V, and Charles VIII was the great-great-grandson of the same king. Hence, they were both in a direct line from Eleanor of Aquitaine.

Finally, Francis I was also a great-great-grandson of Charles V, a first cousin of the previous king. With him we have reached as far as we wish to, having moved from Eleanor's granddaughter, Blanche, through 15 more monarchs to Francis I, who unsuccessfully competed for the throne of Holy Roman Emperor in 1519, when it became vacant with the death of Maximilian I. Francis I was the great(11)-grandson of Eleanor.

Let's relax now with some stories of war. We saw in Chapter 2 that the marriage of Eleanor of Aquitaine to Henry II brought together for England extensive lands in France, more than half of the present-day country. These holdings remained more or less intact from 1154, when Henry and Eleanor gained the thrones, until the early 1200s. At that point, King Philip II Augustus of France recaptured most of this alienated territory from Eleanor's youngest son, King John. In 1259, King Henry III of England (Eleanor's grandson) ratified the Treaty of Paris, signed also by King Louis IX of France (Eleanor's great-grandson), in which he renounced the heritage of his ancestors, with the understanding that English holdings of Ponthieu and

Guyenne (Aquitaine) would be secure.

These sparse land-holdings of the English in France --

compared to what they once had -- prevailed into the 1330s. At

this time, Philip VI was the king of France (1328-1350) and

Edward III was the king of England (1327-1377). Remember

that Philip grabbed the French throne before Edward, who had a

good claim on it, could act. Now beginning in 1337 a war

between the English and the French broke out. This proved to be

the Hundred Years War, which in fact lasted for 116 years.

Early in the war, the English scored two major victories over the French, first at the battle of Crécy in 1346 and then at the battle of Poitiers in 1356. The first victory, a stunning blow to Philip VI and his kingdom, enabled the English to move their troops to Calais in an attempt to capture that fortified city, so strategically located across the channel from Dover. The siege of Calais lasted a year. At that point, the people of Calais, starving, surrendered. Edward III, angry over the time and money spent on this siege -- he was engaged in it himself -- wanted to deal harshly with these obstinate people. But his counselors prevailed on him to soften his demands. He agreed that six of the principal citizens of Calais would come out, their heads and feet bare,

ropes around their necks, with the keys of the town and castle.

Edward declared that he would decide the fate of these men as

he wished.

The six burghers of Calais filed out of the city into an open

space beyond. The king glared at them savagely and ordered that

their heads be chopped off. Right then, his wife, Philippa of

Hainault, "pregnant as she was, humbly threw herself on her

knees before the king and said, weeping: 'Ah, my dear lord,

since I crossed the sea at great danger to myself, you know that I

have never asked a single favor from you. But now I ask you in all humility, in the name of the Son of the Blessed Mary and by the love you bear me, to have mercy on these six men.'"

The king, out of love and respect for his wife, relented and turned over the six burghers to her. This is the incident that impressed Auguste Rodin, 5 1/2 centuries later, to carve his famous Burghers of Calais.

A decade later, after Philip VI had died and had been succeeded by his son, Jean II The Good, the English again handed the French a terrible beating, this time at Maupertuis, six miles southeast of Poitiers. The so-called battle of Poitiers occurred in September, 1356. In eight or nine hours of fighting, the English forces, led by the Black Prince, the eldest son of Edward III, decisively defeated a French army that was at least twice their size. Moreover, the English gained this victory despite having a population to draw on that was only 20 or 25 per cent of France's population, and despite facing also the cream of France's knights and nobles on their best mounts, led by King Jean II and his four teenage sons.

The French were beaten by foot soldiers using long-bows, who could shoot arrows accurately and much more rapidly than the French forces could with their cross-bow weapons. The

French cavalry -- knights and nobles and attendants on

horseback -- were cut down, piled up, and slaughtered by the

successive dark waves of arrows into which they rode.

Essentially, the same outcome had been produced in the

same way at Crécy.

It would be produced for the third time at Agincourt in

1415 -- three similar major defeats of the French in the space of

about 70 years. It is easy to believe from this that the French

were slow learners. But part of the explanation concerns class

structures: knights and nobles on horseback represented a social class far above that of the common foot soldiers, who were

mostly peasants. A higher social class does not easily demote

itself in favor of a lower class. Then, too, nobles on horses ruled

the day from the Battle of Hastings in 1066 -- shown so clearly

in the Bayeux tapestry -- up to the eve of Crécy in 1346. It was

so difficult to believe that this advantage would not continue for

another few hundred years. Moreover, so far as Poitiers was

concerned, Jean II was not a good military strategist, and his

close advisors were sharply divided over how to deal with the

English archers on foot. The result was a fatal hesitation that

sealed the fate of the French. Finally, the English archers were exceptionally well-trained, under royal decree that made them practice for long hours and that furnished them with ample supplies of arrows. The French losses at Poitiers were several thousands killed, including about 2,500 from the nobility.

The English holdings of land in France were greatly increased owing to their military victories at Crécy and Poitiers. But the death of Jean II in 1364 brought his son, Charles V, to the throne, and this French king, by 1380, had reconquered everything but Ponthieu, Calais, and a small territory around Bordeaux and around Bayonne. By that time, Edward III and Philippa were dead. Richard II was the king of England, Charles

V of France would die in that year of 1380, to be succeeded by

his son, Charles VI.

In turn, Charles VII succeeded his father in 1422. The next

son called himself Louis XI, 1461-1483. Now we arrive at

Charles VIII and a story I wish to tell. Charles VIII married

Anne of Brittany in 1491, when he was 21 and she younger.

After seven years of marriage, Anne had given birth to three

sons and one daughter, but they had each succumbed at a very

tender age. Now, in April 1498, at the Château of Amboise,

Anne had once more lost an infant.

Francis I, King of France

Charles VIII, desiring to cheer her up and give her

something else to think about, proposed to her that they go out

and watch a game of tennis (jeu de paume) being played in an

enclosure in the moat of the Château. Anne accepted, although

she knew that the way leading to the enclosure was difficult, and

she still felt weak. Charles took the queen by the hand and led

the way. As they entered the enclosure, Charles banged his head

against "le montant d'une porte basse," which was probably a

lintel, perhaps lowered because work was being done on the

door.

For the moment, the king thought little about it, and the two entered, remained standing, and followed passionately "les échanges rapides des joueurs," when suddenly Charles fell backwards, unconscious. He was carried by the players to the nearest room, which had housed falcons and hence was the dirtiest room of the Château. Since there was no bed there. Charles was placed on a miserable straw pile where "après sept heures d'agonie," he died. He was only 27 years old and without an heir.

The picture, in my mind, of Charles taking Anne by the hand and leading her -- I have to think "lovingly and gently" --

down rather treacherous staircases, without banisters, until they arrived at the fateful door of the tennis court -- this picture is somehow very moving.

A sequel to this story is that Anne became queen again when she married the dead king's second cousin, who was in line for the throne, namely Louis XII, 1462-1515. Louis XII was already married to a sister of the dead king, Jeanne of France. Can you imagine? No wonder everybody is a direct descendant of our Eleanor! Jeanne, however, was sterile, and Louis XII was madly in love with Anne of Brittany. So he got an annulment on the grounds that this woman had been forced on him. He then

108

married Anne, which -- and here is the main point -- also served

to keep Brittany within the French kingdom. In fact there was a

marriage contract between Anne of Brittany and her dead

husband that stipulated that if she became a widow without a

male child, she would marry the next king of France. And so she

did.

Another sequel is that the sterile and discarded Jeanne of

France became a saint. She was a hunchback, had a bad limp,

was wrinkled from head to toe, was sterile, had a violent temper,

tyrannized over others, was despised by her father, and rejected

by her husband. She died at the age of 41. She qualified for sainthood by Rome from the 1600s -- "a model of patience and peace"-- but was canonized only on May 28, 1950.

Okay, pause, take another look. Charles VIII was the young king who died tragically while watching a tennis game. He was the great-great-grandson of Charles V. The great-grandson of Charles V, through a different son, succeeded the young, dead king, as Louis XII. Finally, Louis XII's first cousin came after him, calling himself Francis I. Charles V, was, of course, a direct descendant of Eleanor, and so all the others were, too.

That's the end of the French story. There is no more

Chapter 5
Spain

I am certain that you recall that Eleanor of Aquitaine sent her namesake daughter to Spain to marry King Alfonso VIII of Castile. She was 8 or 9 years old and the year was 1170. Our Eleanor took this very young girl to Bordeaux, and from there she was escorted by others over the Pyrenees to Castile. Eleanor next saw her 30 years later when she, Eleanor, at the age of 78, traveled overland to Castile to fetch one of her granddaughters from this marriage, as a bride for the future Louis VIII of France. In any case, Eleanor of Aquitaine's young Eleanor began the Spanish highway that eventually led to Charles V, in 1519, who was not only king of Spain but also the Holy Roman Emperor. In this chapter, we will travel this Spanish highway that starts with our Eleanor and ends with Charles V.

We'll start in the usual way with the usual information. The listing below shows the kings and queens of "Spain", starting from our Eleanor's young daughter, also named Eleanor, who became the queen of Castile. The list ends with Charles V.

King or Queen.	Birth-Death.	Reign Years.	Relationship
Eleanor.	1162-1211?	1170-1214.	Eleanor's daughter
Enrique I.	1204-1217.	1214-1217.	Son of young Eleanor
Berenguela.	1180?-1246.	1188?-1230.	Daughter of young El.
Fernando III.	1199-1252.	1217-1252.	Son
		1230-1252	
Alfonso X.	1221-1284.	1252-1284.	Son
Sancho IV.	1257-1295.	1284-1296	Son
Fernando IV.	1285-1312.	1296-1312.	Son
Alfonso XI.	1311-1350.	1312-1350.	Son
Pedro I.	1334-1369.	1350-1369.	Son
Enrique II.	1333-1379.	1369-1379.	Illegitimate half brother
Juan I.	1358-1390.	1379-1390.	Son

113

Enrique III.	1379-1406.	1390-1406.	Son
Juan II.	1405-1454.	1406-1454.	Son
Enrique IV.	1425-1474.	1454-1474.	Son
Isabella.	1451-1504.	1474-1504.	Half-Sister
Juana.	1479-1555.	1504-1516	Daughter
Charles V.	1500-1558.	1516-1558.	Son

Enrique I and Berenguela were children of young Eleanor. The former, as king, was only 13 when he died, and so he left no heir. He is included here but not really necessary for our story. Fernando III was the king of Castile when his uncle, Enrique I died. Fernando III became the king of Leon when his mother,

Berenguela, died. Enrique II, though illegitimate, was still the

son of Alfonso XI.

I am using Spanish names -- Enrique and Fernando, for

example, instead of Henry and Ferdinand -- but I am keeping

Charles V because he is so widely known by that name.

Young Eleanor became the queen of Castile when, aged 8

or 9, she married Alfonso VIII, king of Castile in 1170. One of

their daughters, Berenguela, was married, perhaps at the age of

8, to King Alfonso IX of Leon in 1188. Their son, Fernando III,

115

eventually inherited both Castile and Leon, reuniting the two lands under one ruler.

The first marriage of Fernando III to Beatrice of Swabia produced the next king of Castile and Leon, Alfonso X, who reigned for 32 years, from 1252 to 1284. This marriage produced nine other children, all of whom may have had wonderful lives, but we can push them all to the side because we need only Alfonso X. Incidentally, we noted in Chapter 3 that a daughter of Fernando III's second marriage was married to King Edward I of England. Okay, back to Alfonso X, king of Castile and Leon from 1252 to 1284. His son was Sancho IV, followed by Fernando IV. This takes us to about 1300, and we can note that Fernando IV was the great(4)-grandson of Eleanor of Aquitaine.

From Fernando IV to Charles V is more or less a straight shot, but there are a few bumps along the way. Son followed father most of the time, but Enrique II was an illegitimate son of Alfonso XI and hence the illegitimate half-brother of Pedro I. For our purposes, in establishing the Eleanor highway through Spain, this makes no difference, for Enrique II was indeed the son of Alfonso XI -- he simply had a mistress -- who himself carried the genes of Eleanor of Aquitaine. The other bump in the

117

highway comes with Isabella, who was the half-sister of the preceding king, Enrique IV. But Isabella was the daughter of Juan II. Isabella's own daughter, Juana, carried the Eleanor highway farther, and we have reached the end of our road with her son, Charles V, king of Spain and Holy Roman Emperor.

Juana married Philip, son of Maximilian I, in 1496. She gave birth to Charles in 1500, and, upon her mother's death in 1504, she became queen. However, Juana's husband, Philip I, died suddenly in 1506, and this unexpected death aggravated Juana's mental instability. At her father's death in 1516, Juana's son, Charles, became Spain's monarch with his mother, but she spent the rest of her tormented life in the convent of Santa Clara

in Tordesillas. So her reign effectively ended in 1516, but she

had the title of queen until her death 39 years later. She lived to

be 76 years old.

Alfonso XI, who lived from 1311 to only 1350, reigned

during the time of Edward II and Edward III of England, and

Philip IV, his sons, and Philip VI of France. In Spain, the Moors

had been driven into the southeast corner of the country, but it

would be more than another century before they were finally

expelled totally. Hence, Alfonso XI, in mid-stream so to speak,

while fighting the Moors and making some gains against them, mostly concentrated on re-establishing royal authority after his

weak predecessors had yielded much ground to the aristocracy.

Alfonso XI is in Donizetti's opera, La Favorita. In the

opera, he captures Sevilla and the Alcazar from the Moors. In

fact, Sevilla was taken in 1248, 100 years earlier. The Alcazar

was restored and enlarged by Alfonso's son, Pedro I.

Alfonso died at the young age of 40. He was succeeded by

his son, Pedro I, 16 at the time. Alfonso XI's mistress was slain

by Pedro's supporters and at his instigation and the eldest

(illegitimate) son by this union, furiously struck back against his half-brother for that foul deed. To make matters worse, Pedro

deserted his wife for a young lady whose family members

received many favors from the king, all of this angering the

nobility. The civil war that followed involved not only Castile --

and Aragon -- but France and England as well. The combatants

in the Hundred Years War, 1337-1453, now used Spain as their

battlefield.

Charles I, King of Spain and
Charles V, Holy Roman Emperor

Pedro I initially gained the upper hand, but Enrique enlisted the support of Aragon and France (mid-1360s), while England temporarily backed Pedro I and the Castilians. After England withdrew its support, Enrique decisively defeated Pedro in 1368, and, after slaying Pedro himself, Enrique II became the next king.

The son of Enrique II, Juan I, succeeded his father in 1379 and reigned until 1390. During these years, both England and Portugal were involved in fighting Juan I, king of Castile and Leon. One of Edward III's sons, John of Gaunt, married a daughter of Pedro I. So that put him against Pedro's arch-enemy,

Enrique II and his son, the present king, Juan I. Moreover, by his

first marriage, John of Gaunt had a daughter who married the

king of Portugal. So John of Gaunt now had a Portuguese army

on his side. It was John against Juan, and Juan won. You won't

believe this, but Juan I's son, who called himself Enrique III,

married a daughter of John of Gaunt -- the man his father had

been battling for years. Ready? And this daughter was of course

a direct descendant of Eleanor of Aquitaine. Naturally --

daughter of a son of Edward III of England, and from there

directly up to Eleanor. Voilà. This last word is to bring the

French into the picture along with the English, Spanish, and Portuguese.

Enrique III's rule was weak, allowing the aristocracy to gain wealth and power at the expense of the crown. When Enrique died in 1406, his son -- the future Juan II -- was only one year old. An uncle acted as regent, but for the next half century of Juan II's rule the aristocracy fought among itself and against the crown for domination within the existing system. Juan II's first marriage to Maria of Aragon produced the next king, Enrique IV, whose reign lasted two decades, 1454 to 1474, during which internal turmoil between the high nobility and the

crown persisted.

Enrique IV left no male heir, but he did have a daughter,

Juana, whom many people felt could not possibly be his, given

his "sexual perversion and impotence". She was called Juana la

Beltraneja to reflect her supposed father, probably without

justification. This daughter later married a Portuguese king,

Afonso V (1432-1481).

So much for Enrique IV. To continue along the Eleanor

highway in Spain, we now have to return to Enrique IV's father,

Juan II of Castile. The second marriage of Juan II to Isabel of Portugal, brought forth two children -- Alfonso and Isabella. Alfonso died young, several years before the end of Enrique IV's reign. That left the girl, who was destined to become Queen Isabella I of Castile and Leon. But it was not easy. When Enrique IV died in 1474, a five-year struggle began between those supporting Juana la Beltraneja, the daughter of the king, and the supporters of Isabella, the half-sister of the king.

We are talking about Enrique IV. Juana was his daughter. Isabella was his half-sister because they had the same father but different mothers. For five years the clashes continued between

Juana and Isabella before Isabella's military forces, beefed up by

the Aragonese, won out. In 1479, Isabella married Fernando of

Aragon, her second cousin. This marriage united Castile, Leon,

and Aragon. It also produced another Juana -- that's what

Isabella named her daughter, after her former bitterest enemy! --

but this one turned out to be Juana the Mad. Nevertheless, Juana

the Mad eventually gave birth to Charles V, king of Spain and

Holy Roman Emperor.

You will be amazed and totally flabbergasted to learn that

Charles V was a direct descendant of Eleanor of Aquitaine. And here is more, over the top: so was Juana the Mad. Could there

have been loco genes from Eleanor? Doesn't seem possible.

Chapter 6
Portugal

I noted Portugal a few times in the previous chapter. Portugal now belongs on our stage. Eleanor, her eight children, and her second husband, Henry II, king of England, are on one side. On the other side, 3 1/2 centuries later, are the four monarchs: Henry VIII, king of England; Francis I, king of France; Charles I, king of Spain; and Maximilian I, Holy Roman Emperor. The year on their side is 1519. Now we add to these four Manuel I, king of Portugal, 1469-1521. In this chapter, we will travel from our Eleanor to Manuel I, and of course we will find that Manuel I is a direct descendant of Eleanor of Aquitaine.

We will begin again when Eleanor of Aquitaine sent her very young daughter, in 1170, also named Eleanor, to the court of Castile to marry Alfonso VIII, who became the king of Castile in 1158 at the age of 3. Now he was 15 and married to an 8 year-old. Eventually, the pair had three daughters, Berenguela, Urraca, and Blanche. Berenguela was married to Alfonso IX of Leon, at around 8 years old. Blanche, you will remember, was brought back to France by our Eleanor to wed the future Louis VIII. That leaves Urraca. She was married to the heir of the

Portuguese throne, Afonso II. This began the journey of the genes of our Eleanor through Portugal, down finally to Manuel I. Urraca was a granddaughter of Eleanor, which is our starting point, and there were 12 kings along the way to Manuel. They are listed below with the usual information.

Urraca, Queen of Portugal

King.	Birth-Death.	Reign Years.	Relationship
Afonso II.	1185-1223.	1211-1223.	Son; married Urraca
Sancho II.	1205-1246.	1223-1246.	Son
Afonso III.	1210-1279.	1246-1279.	Brother
Dinis.	1261-1325.	1279-1325.	Son
Afonso IV.	1291--357!	1325-1357.	Son
Pedro I.	1320-1367.	1357-1367	Son
Fernando.	1345-1383.	1367-1383.	Son
João I.	1357-1433.	1384-1433.	Half-Brother
Duarte.	1391-1438.	1433-1438.	Son
Afonso V.	1432-1481.	1438-1481.	Son
João II.	1453-1495.	1481-1495.	Son
Manuel I.	1469-1521.	1495-1521.	First Cousin

If you look at the relationship of each king to his predecessor, everything seems clear, except João I. However, he was the son of Pedro I, as was Fernando, but each had a different mother. Since Pedro I was in Eleanor's family, so were the two sons. Manuel I and João II were both grandsons of King Duarte, but through two different sons of Duarte. That made them first cousins, as the table above shows. Afonso V was of course one of those sons. The other son did not reign.

The table shows that Manuel I was born in 1469 and died in 1521. He was the king of Portugal from 1495 until his death. This was a period during which Portugal's overseas empire expanded enormously and much wealth flowed into the country.

During these years, Vasco da Gama sailed to India; Cabral

reached Brazil on his way to India; parts of Africa, including the

Congo and Guinea, were explored; Goa and Malacca were

conquered; and China was visited, with a base established at

Macao. These overseas explorations had been set in motion by

Manuel's great-grandfather, João I, who took Ceuta in North

Africa from the Moors in 1415. Subsequently, several other

African ports were added to Portugal's overseas possessions.

Henry the Navigator, a son of João I, distinguished himself at

Ceuta and later headed the exploration of the coast of west

Africa. These led to Vasco da Gama's and Cabral's exploits that culminated in Portuguese domination of the spice trade.

Manuel himself came along at the right time to reap much of the harvest. However, his main interest and focus were on these sailing ventures and not on European or even Iberian politics. Portugal's destiny, he felt, was overseas; it was not as a competitor in Europe's quarrels. His position was vindicated in that the foreign exploits of the Portuguese were hailed in all European courts, and Manuel was given the greatest respect and honors by other royalties.

Manuel was married three times. His first two wives were daughters of Isabella and Fernando, monarchs of Spain, and his third wife was the sister of Emperor Charles V -- both the sister and her brother were grandchildren of Isabella and Fernando. Manuel had at least 13 children, only three of whom died as small infants. His first wife succumbed while giving birth to his first child. His second wife produced 10 children in 17 years. After her death in 1517, Manuel married Eleanor -- we'll never run out of Eleanors -- Charles V's sister, and had two more children by her, in a marriage that lasted only three years to Manuel's death.

Manuel had at first arranged a marriage of Eleanor to his son, João. But he suddenly decided to marry Eleanor himself. Verdi's opera, Don Carlo, has the same theme, a true one, too, set in Spain under Philip II and his son, Don Carlo.

Manuel's son, João, who lost this one, succeeded his father as king a few years later. Manuel's eldest daughter, Isabella, married Charles V -- and that proved to be a very happy marriage, as I already noted in Chapter 5.

Eleanor of Aquitaine would have been proud of this great (8)-grandson, this Portuguese king. Not only was he earnestly and actively interested in a Crusade against the Moors, and not only did he administer land far beyond his own realm -- similar in both respects to Eleanor -- but he was a life-long lover of poetry and music, a talented student of architecture, and a connoisseur of visual arts. He lived surrounded by musicians, and his chapel had the finest choir in Europe. His was a highly cultured court. Eleanor probably would not have been surprised to find that one of her granddaughters, who was a queen of Portugal and who had come from a Castilian court brimming with artists, had somehow initiated the transfer of this cultural heritage down to Manuel some 300 years later.

Chapter 7

The First Grandmother of Europe

It is Eleanor of Aquitaine who has been called the "grandmother of Europe," as a way of acknowledging her many descendants over the centuries in numerous royal courts of Europe. I have discussed the major ones, but there were several others. Also, since Eleanor, a few other queens have been assigned that title, but, for sure, Eleanor can be called the first grandmother of Europe.

She got off to a rousing, royal start with nine of her great-grandchildren, all of whom were kings or queens. Three -- perhaps four-- of them were born before her own death. The listing below is by date of birth.

Great-Grandchild.	Title.	Birth-Death Dates
Alix (Alice).	Queen of Cyprus.	1194?-1246
Fernando III.	King of Castile and Leon.	1199-1252
Thibaut I.	King of Navarre.	1201-1252?
Sancho II.	King of Portugal.	1205?-1246
Louis IX.	King of France.	1214-1270
Charles I.	King of Naples, Sicily, And Jerusalem	1227-1285
Edward I.	King of England.	1239-1307
Alexander III.	King of Scotland.	1241-1286
Margaret.	Queen of Scotland.	1246?-1290?

Alix and Thibaut I were offspring from Eleanor's first marriage to Louis VII, king of France. Eleanor's two girls, whom she lost to Louis VII when their marriage was annulled, were sent by the French court to two brothers, one the count of Champagne and the other the count of Blois. Both girls were raised in those courts and then married in 1164. The older, Marie, had two sons, one of whom produced Alix, Queen of Cyprus, and the other of whom had Thibaut I, King of Navarre.

Fernando III, you may remember from Chapter 5, re-unified Castile and Leon. He was the son of Berenguela, a granddaughter of our Eleanor. Sancho II, King of Portugal, was the son of Urraca, who was a sister of Berenguela. And Louis IX, Saint Louis, was the son of Blanche, another sister of Berenguela and Urraca. So these three kings -- from Spain, Portugal, and France -- were sons of the three sisters from a remarkable Castilian court, the queen of which was the namesake daughter of Eleanor of Aquitaine. You may also recall that Eleanor visited that court in 1200 at the age of 78, before the airplane or the automobile were invented. There she saw her daughter for the first time in 30 years.

Next in the listing, Charles I was a brother of Louis IX. He was given a handful of titles: King of Sicily, King of Naples,

King of Jerusalem, count of Maine, count of Anjou, count of

Provence. Edward I of England was the son of Henry III and the

grandson of King John, our Eleanor's last child.

Eleanor's great-grandchildren also included a queen and

king of Scotland, married to each other and named Margaret and

Alexander III. Henry III and his wife, Eleanor of Provence,

produced Margaret, while Alexander III was the grandson of

Eleanor's last child, King John I.

These nine great-grandchildren of Eleanor sent her genes to

Cyprus, Navarre, Spain, England, France, Scotland, Naples and

Sicily, Jerusalem, Portugal, Burgundy, and the Holy Roman Empire. As you can guess, there are many more good stories to tell, but they will have to wait for another day.

We started with Eleanor and her brood on one side of a stage. On the other side were Henry VIII of England, Francis I of France, Charles I of Spain, and Maximilian I, Holy Roman Emperor. The year was 1519. When Maximilian died that year, the other three vied for his throne. Charles I won it and became Charles V, Holy Roman Emperor, as well as Charles I, King of Spain.

Francis I never, never forgave Charles for imposing this humiliating defeat on him, and this wound, which remained open, contributed to the several wars between the two over the following 25 years. In the end, Spain was the winner, with a final defeat of the French in 1559, a year after the death of Charles V.

If we go far beyond our terminal year of 1519, right up to the present day, we find that Queen Elizabeth II is the great(24)-granddaughter of Eleanor of Aquitaine, King Juan Carlos of Spain is her great(26)-grandson, and the count of Paris, Henri d'Orleans, who died at the age of 90 in 1999, was Eleanor's great(23)-grandson. I record these facts without comment,

without further investigation, but with awe.

About the Author

The most important thing to know about John Gurley is that he is ninety-six years old going on one hundred. He has been retired from his position of professor of economics at Stanford University for twenty-eight years, long enough to learn hundreds of new things. He has written four brief books about caring for his wife, Yvette, during her stay in a dementia unit in Palo Alto, California, books that were published by AuthorHouse in the last few years and which have received twenty-four five-star reviews.

Prior to his twenty-eight years at Stanford, Gurley taught economics at Princeton University and did research with his wife, who is also an economist, at Brookings Institution in Washington, DC. John and Yvette, along with Professor Edward Shaw, completed a major work in 1960, with the publication of Money in a Theory of Finance.

Since his retirement in 1987, John Gurley has studied early French and English histories as backgrounds to his later work on Eleanor of Aquitaine. He is presently living alone—since the death of his wife in December 2014—in a large retirement community located in Palo Alto, on the edge of Stanford University's huge landholdings.

Printed in the United States
By Bookmasters